This book belongs to:

....

My FIRST Prayers

Additional prayers by Meryl Doney and Jan Payne
Cover illustrated by Emily Dove
Internals illustrated by Charlotte Cooke, Emily Dove,
Chiara Fiorentino, Madison Mastrangelo, Alessandra Psacharopulo,
Luisa Uribe, and Ben Whitehouse
Designed by Duck Egg Blue and Karissa Santos
Edited by Lily Holland
Consultant: Nicki Copeland
Production by Juliet Fountain

Every effort has been made to acknowledge the contributors to this book.
If we have made any errors, we will be pleased to rectify them in future editions.

This edition published by Parragon Books Ltd in 2016 and distributed by

Parragon Inc.
440 Park Avenue South, 13th Floor
New York, NY 10016
www.parragon.com

ISBN 978-1-4748-1480-5

Printed in China

My FIRST Prayers

Bath • New York • Cologne • Melbourne • Delhi
Hong Kong • Shenzhen • Singapore

Contents

My World Is Wonderful

All things bright and beautiful,
All creatures, great and small,
All things wise and wonderful,
The Lord God made them all.

Each little flower that opens,
Each little bird that sings,
He made their glowing colors,
He made their tiny wings.

The tall trees in the greenwood,
The meadows where we play,
The rushes by the water
We gather every day.

He gave us eyes to see them,
And lips that we might tell
How great is God Almighty,
Who has made all things well.

CECIL FRANCES ALEXANDER (1818–1895)

Thank You, God, for showing me
The perfect beauty of a tree.
I didn't know a tree could be
Remarkable, like You and me.

Dear God,
Bless our nets as we cast and trawl;
The ocean is deep and our ship is small.

13

For flowers that bloom about our feet,
Father, we thank Thee.
For tender grass so fresh, so sweet,
Father, we thank Thee.
For the bird and hum of bee,
For all things fair we hear or see,
Father in heaven, we thank Thee.

RALPH WALDO EMERSON (1803–1882)

For air and sunshine, pure and sweet,
We thank our heavenly Father.
For grass that grows beneath our feet,
We thank our heavenly Father.
For lovely flowers and blossoms gay,
For trees and woods in bright array,
For birds that sing in joyful lay,
We thank our heavenly Father.

Tomorrow is a special day—
My family and I are going away!
We're going where there's sand and sea,
And ball games we can play with glee;
Where donkeys give rides on the beach,
And seagulls fly just out of reach;
Where Mom's skirt billows in the breeze,
And Dad gets wet up to his knees!
Thank You, God, for such good things,
For rocks and boats and rubber rings,
For sand and shells and sky and sun,
For the simple joy of having fun.

For this new morning and its light,
For rest and shelter of the night,
For health and food, for love and friends,
For every gift Your goodness sends,
We thank You, gracious Lord.

God made the world so broad and grand,
Filled with blessings from His hand.
He made the sky so high and blue,
And made the little children, too.

Dear God,
Thank You for the sun so bright,
Which fills the world with dazzling light.
And thank You for the muffled sound
When snow lies thickly on the ground.

A special thanks for gentle rain,
Which helps the grass grow green again.
But please, God, send the wind, I pray,
So I can fly my kite today.

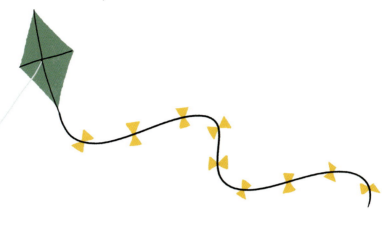

The year's at the spring;
The day's at the morn;
Morning's at seven;
The hill-side's dew-pearled;
The lark's on the wing;
The snail's on the thorn;
God's in His heaven—
All's right with the world!

ROBERT BROWNING (1812–1889)

For all the rich autumnal glories spread—
The flaming pageant of the ripening woods,
The fiery gorse, the heather-purpled hills;
The rustling leaves that fly before the wind
And lie below the hedgerows whispering;
For meadows silver-white with hoary dew;
The first crisp breath of wonder in the air,
We thank You, Lord.

O, thought I!
What a beautiful thing
God has made winter to be
By stripping trees
And letting us see
Their shape and forms.
What a freedom does it seem
To give them to the storms.

DOROTHY WORDSWORTH (1771–1855)

Joy to the world!
The Lord is come;
Let Earth receive her King;
Let every heart
Prepare Him room,
And heav'n and nature sing,
And heav'n and nature sing,
And heav'n, and heav'n
And nature sing.

Joy to the world!
The Savior reigns;
Let men their songs employ,
While fields and floods,
Rocks, hills and plains
Repeat the sounding joy,
Repeat the sounding joy,
Repeat, repeat
The sounding joy.

Isaac Watts (1674–1748)

Praise the Lord! Ye heavens adore Him,
Praise Him, angels in the height!
Sun and Moon, rejoice before Him,
Praise Him, all ye stars and light.

JOHN KEMPTHORNE (1775–1838)

All things praise Thee, Lord most high!
Heaven and Earth and sea and sky!
Time and space are praising Thee!
All things praise Thee; Lord, may we!

GEORGE WILLIAM CONDER (1821–1874)

God bless the field and bless the furrow,
Stream and branch and rabbit burrow.
Bless the minnow, bless the whale,
Bless the rainbow and the hail,
Bless the nest and bless the leaf,
Bless the righteous and the thief,
Bless the wing and bless the fin,
Bless the air I travel in,
Bless the mill and bless the mouse,
Bless the miller's bricken house,
Bless the earth and bless the sea,
God bless you and God bless me.

Josie is my best friend;
She's never rude or cross.

Jamie is the tallest;
He thinks he is the boss.

Jason wears a white shirt
And gets his math all right.

Alice is the sweetest;
Her curls are small and tight.

All my friends are special;
They mean a lot to me.
And Jesus is my friend as well,
Because he cares for me.

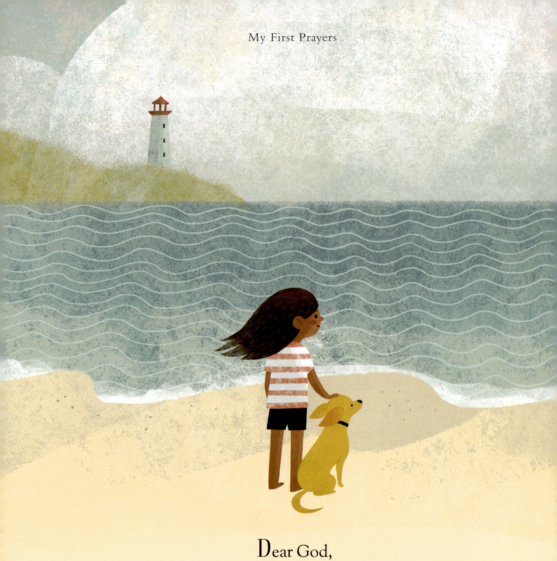

Dear God,
I love to be on the beach
Where the sand meets the sea.
It reminds me what a wonderful
world You've made.

I can look far out,
Where the sea meets the sky,
And know that there's a wonderful world out there.
Perhaps, one day,
I'll go traveling and see the world.

Thank You for flowers;
Thank You for trees;
Thank You for grasses
That toss in the breeze.

Thank You for vegetables;
Thank You for spice;
Thank You for everything
That makes food taste nice.

Thank You, dear Father,
For all things that grow,
In sunshine and rain,
And the glowing rainbow.

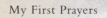

I love to see the raindrops
Splashing on the sidewalks;
I love to see the sunlight
Twinkling in the rain;
I love to see the wind-gusts
Drying up the raindrops;
I love to feel the sunshine
Coming out again.

Thank You for the thunderstorm,
Thank You for the wind and rain,
And thank You for the sunshine
Coming out again.

Wide as the world,
(spread arms wide)

Deep as the sea,
(point down deep)

High as the sky,
(point up high)

Is Your love for me.
(hug yourself)

God bless our school.
Help our teachers.
Strengthen the principal.
And bless all the children.
Amen

I have
quiet friends,
noisy friends,
funny ones and sad,
many friends,
few friends,
sensible and mad,
good friends,
naughty friends,
tall friends and short;
thank You, God,
for giving me
friends of every sort.

When I travel in a bus,
I see the streets and houses.
When I go in a train,
I see the fields and hills.
When I fly in an airplane,
I can see the whole country.

If I could go up in a rocket,
I would see the whole world.
Thank You, God, for travel.
It shows me what a great world
You have made.

39

God Bless the Animals

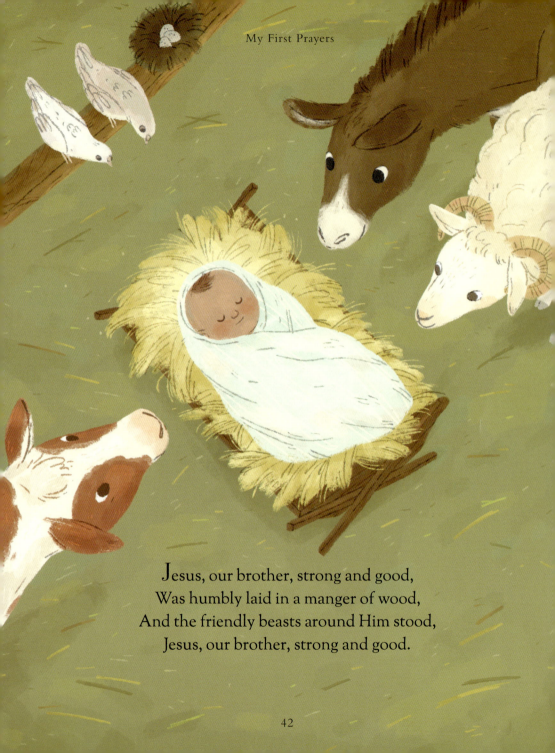

Jesus, our brother, strong and good,
Was humbly laid in a manger of wood,
And the friendly beasts around Him stood,
Jesus, our brother, strong and good.

"I," said the donkey, shaggy and brown,
"I carried His mother uphill and down;
I carried her safely to Bethlehem town,
I," said the donkey, shaggy and brown.

"I," said the cow, all white and red,
"I gave Him my manger for His bed;
I gave Him my hay to pillow His head,
I," said the cow, all white and red.

"I," said the sheep with the curly horn,
"I gave Him my wool for His blanket warm;
He wore my coat on Christmas morn,
I," said the sheep with the curly horn.

"I," said the dove, from the rafters high,
"Cooed Him to sleep, my mate and I;
We cooed Him to sleep, my mate and I,
I," said the dove, from the rafters high.

And every beast, by some good spell,
In the stable dark was glad to tell
Of the gift he gave Immanuel,
The gift he gave Immanuel.

Twelfth-century carol

Thank You, God, for giving us
The hippo and rhinoceros;
For crazy monkeys, brash and loud;
Giraffes with heads stuck in the clouds.
Thanks for parrots, bold and bright,
And zebras smart in black and white;
For elephants with giant feet,
And anteaters so trim and neat.
I wouldn't want the world to be
Empty except for You and me.

God Bless the Animals

The little cares that fretted me,
I lost them yesterday,
Among the fields above the sea,
Among the winds at play,
Among the lowing herds,
The rustling of the trees,
Among the singing of the birds,
The humming of the bees.

The foolish fears of what might pass,
I cast them away,
Among the clover-scented grass,
Among the new-mown hay,
Among the hushing of the corn,
Where the drowsy poppies nod,
Where ill thoughts die and good are born—
Out in the fields with God.

Louise Imogen Guiney (1861–1920)

Little lamb, who made thee?
Dost thou know who made thee?
Gave thee life and bade thee feed
By the stream and over the mead;
Gave thee clothing of delight,
Softest clothing, woolly, bright;
Gave thee such a tender voice
Making all the vales rejoice?

Little lamb, who made thee?
Dost thou know who made thee?

Little lamb, I'll tell thee;
Little lamb, I'll tell thee;
He is called by thy name,
For He calls himself a Lamb;
He is meek and He is mild,
He became a little child.
I a child and thou a lamb,
We are called by His name,

Little lamb, God bless thee!
Little lamb, God bless thee!

WILLIAM BLAKE (1757–1827)

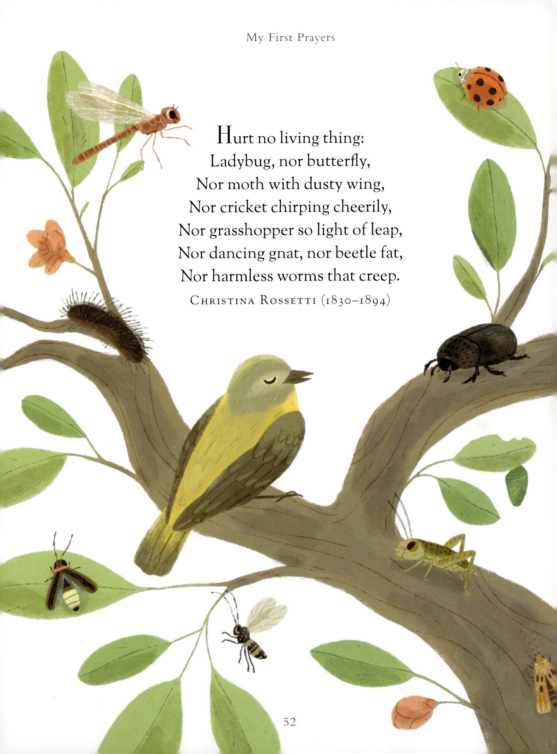

Hurt no living thing:
Ladybug, nor butterfly,
Nor moth with dusty wing,
Nor cricket chirping cheerily,
Nor grasshopper so light of leap,
Nor dancing gnat, nor beetle fat,
Nor harmless worms that creep.

CHRISTINA ROSSETTI (1830–1894)

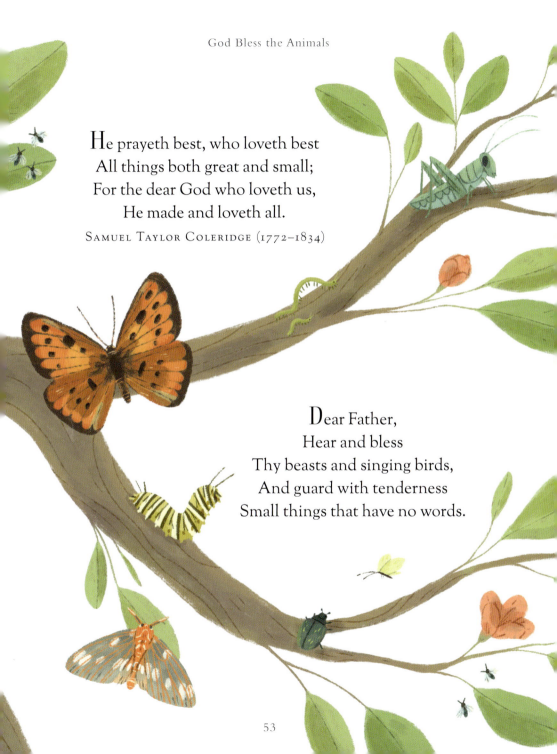

He prayeth best, who loveth best
All things both great and small;
For the dear God who loveth us,
He made and loveth all.

SAMUEL TAYLOR COLERIDGE (1772–1834)

Dear Father,
Hear and bless
Thy beasts and singing birds,
And guard with tenderness
Small things that have no words.

Beetles are funny;
ants are, too;
flies have fantastic wings.
Sometimes, I like them,
so my prayer is,
"Thank You, God, for the smallest things."

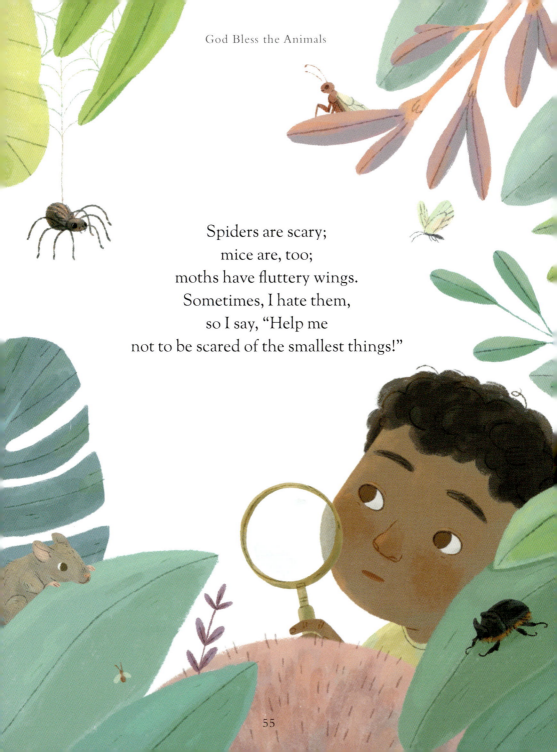

Spiders are scary;
mice are, too;
moths have fluttery wings.
Sometimes, I hate them,
so I say, "Help me
not to be scared of the smallest things!"

When dogs bark and hamsters squeak,
Are they really trying to speak?
When hens and roosters cluck and crow,
Are they really in the know?
Dear God, do animals talk to You
And tell You what they'd like to do?
For, if they can't, I'd like to say,
Please watch over them today.

Loving Shepherd of Thy sheep,
Keep Thy lambs, in safety keep;
Nothing can Thy power withstand;
None that can pluck them from Thy hand.

Jane Eliza Leeson (1807–1882)

To all the humble beasts there be,
To all the birds on land and sea,
Great Spirit, sweet protection give
That free and happy they may live!

God bless the animals
Great and small,
And help us learn
To love them all.

Please listen to this special prayer,
And if I start to cry
It's because my budgie's ill
And I think he's going to die.
Nothing lives forever,
This is something that I know.
But even though I know it,
I wish it wasn't so.

Please, God,
You know how much we love *(pet's name)*
And now *(pet's name)* is not very well.
Please help us to look after *(pet's name)*,
Help the vet to know how to treat *(pet's name)*
And, if possible, make *(pet's name)* better again.
Amen

Dear God,
Our pets are very special.
They give us love and many happy hours.
They teach us how to love and look after them.
They are our friends.
They let us know we're not alone.

So, when they die, we are sad inside.
Help us in our sadness to remember
all the good things about our pets
and to thank You for them.
Amen

Thank You for My Food

Thank You, God,
that I can break
my night-time fast
with breakfast.
What a great way
to start a day!
Amen

Munch, munch, munch,
Thank You for our lunch.

Dear God above,
For all Your love
and for our meal,
we thank You.

Thank You for my dinner;
Thank You for my friends;
Thank You for my family
And love that never ends.

For what we are about to receive,
May the Lord make us truly thankful.
Amen

Bless us, O Lord, and these Thy gifts,
Which of Thy bounty we are about to receive,
Through Christ our Lord.
Amen

I pray that ordinary bread
Be just as nice as cake;
I pray that I could fall asleep
As easy as I wake.

School lunches can taste nasty;
School lunches can taste nice.
But I love my school lunches;
I could eat them twice!

Some days, I eat up everything;
Sometimes, I like to share.
Thank You for school lunches, God,
Because my friends are there.

Pizzas and burgers; a plate of hot dogs;
Barbecued chicken that everyone hogs!

Jello and ice cream; a big birthday cake;
Gingerbread cookies that I helped to make.

These are the things that we all love to eat.
Thank You, dear Father, for each tasty treat.

Oh, the Lord is good to me,
And so I thank the Lord
For giving me the things I need,
The sun, the rain, and the apple seed.
Oh, the Lord is good to me.

JOHN "APPLESEED" CHAPMAN (1774–1845)

Cows make milk
And bees make honey.
Farmers cut corn
When it's sunny.
Plums and apples
Grow on trees.
And in Dad's garden
Are beans and peas.
Thank You, God,
For the food I eat,
For fruit and milk,
And bread and meat.
If it were not for
These gifts from You,
I really don't know what we'd do!

All this world is God's own field,
Fruit unto His praise to yield;
Wheat and tares together sown,
Unto joy or sorrow grown;
First the blade and then the ear,
Then the full corn shall appear:
Lord of the harvest, grant that we
Wholesome grain and pure may be.

HENRY ALFORD (1810–1871)

Red tomato,
Orange carrot,
Yellow pepper,
Lettuce green,
Beetroot that has blue and purple,
Indigo and violet sheen.
Thank You, God, that in my salad
Rainbow colors can be seen.

Here are the apples;
Here the pears,
Crusty bread,
And cream eclairs;
Potatoes and onions,
Barley and rye,
Honey in pots,
And rhubarb pie;
Berries and cherries
And bales of hay.
Thanks be for the harvest
God gave us today.

Father, we thank Thee for this food,
For health and strength and all things good.
May others all these blessings share,
And hearts be grateful everywhere.

Thank You, God,
For this day,
This family
And this food.
Amen

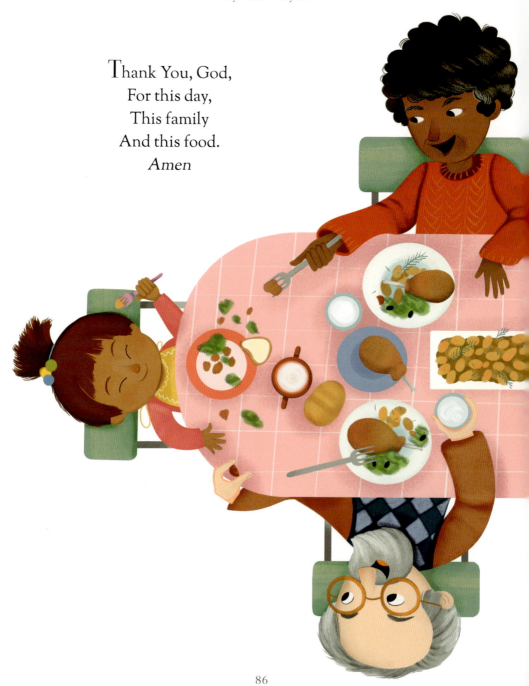

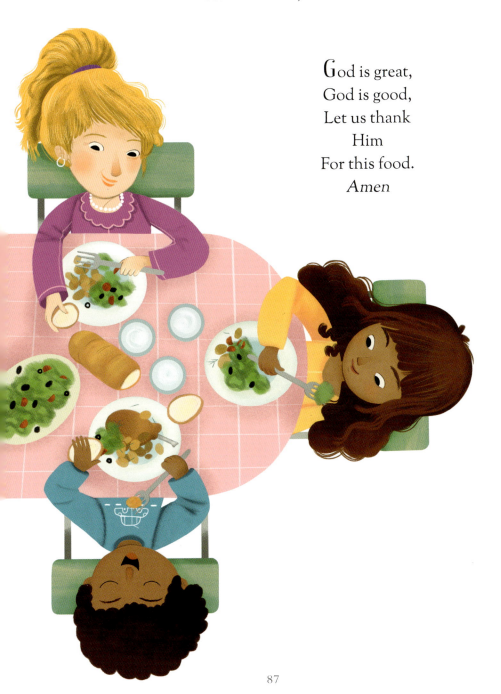

God is great,
God is good,
Let us thank
Him
For this food.
Amen

Jesus fed the multitude
On five loaves and two fishes.
We don't know how He did it,
But, Jesus, bless these dishes!

Some hae meat and canna eat,
And some wad eat that want it;
But we hae meat and we can eat,
And sae the Lord be thankit.

ROBERT BURNS (1759–1796)

Thank You for the precious food
I eat three times a day.
Some children eat just once a week,
So, for them, I pray.
I wish that I could help them,
But I don't know what to do.
Please, God, will You make sure
That they have three meals, too?

May we who have much
Remember those who have little.

May we who are full
Remember those who are hungry.

May we who are loved
Remember those who are lonely.

May we who are safe
Remember those who are in danger.

May we who have so much
Learn to share.

Look After My Family

God bless all those that I love.
God bless all those that love me.
God bless all those that love those that I love,
And all those that love those that love me.

FROM AN OLD NEW ENGLAND SAMPLER

Jesus said,
"Let the little children come to me,
for the kingdom of God
belongs to such as these."

MATTHEW 19:14; MARK 10:14; LUKE 18:16

God bless you,
God bless me,
And keep us safe
As safe can be.

God bless Mom and Dad
For all the good times we have had;
For vacations, birthdays, Christmas fun;
For games and races that I won!

For afternoons spent in the park;
For watching fireworks after dark;
For all the stories they have read
At night, when I go up to bed.

Keep them safe, oh Lord, I pray,
So I can love them every day.

Once, I was a baby;
I used to wear a bib—
But now there's someone else
Sleeping in my crib!
Mom says it's my new brother.
He's very small and sweet,
With hands the size of daisies
And very smooth, pink feet.
I think I'm going to like him
And I know that he'll like me.
God, won't it be terrific
When I can hold him on my knee?

Look After My Family

We've got a new baby.
It's part of our family now.
When it holds my hand
and when it smiles at me,
I like it very much.

We've got a new baby.
It's hungry all the time.
When it makes a smell,
and cries and cries,
I don't like it at all.

Thank You for our new baby.
On bad days and good;
It's part of our family now
and I love it.

Lord, help us to remember that
Love is patient, love is kind.
It does not boast, it is not proud.
It is not envious or self-seeking.
It is not angry, but forgiving.
Love does not lie, but rejoices in truth.
It always protects, it always trusts.
It always hopes, it always tries.
Love never fails.

1 CORINTHIANS 13

Dear God,
I do love my brother,
But I don't always like him.
Sometimes, we fight
And do mean things to each other.
Help me to remember that,
Even when I don't like him,
I still love him.
Amen

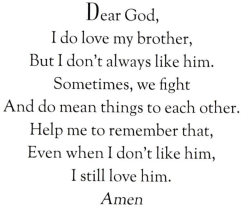

Dear God,
You won't be pleased
With what I did today.
My sister tried to kiss me,
But I turned my face away.
Please tell her that I love her
And I'm really going to try
To be a lot more loving,
But it's hard because I'm shy.

Thank You for Nan,
Who does what she can
When we go to her place.
Thank You for Grandpa,
Who knows where the candies are
And always says grace.
Thank You for visits
And all kinds of treats.
Thank You for walking
Down different streets.
Thank You for good times
Wherever we roam.
But most of all, God,
Thank You for home.

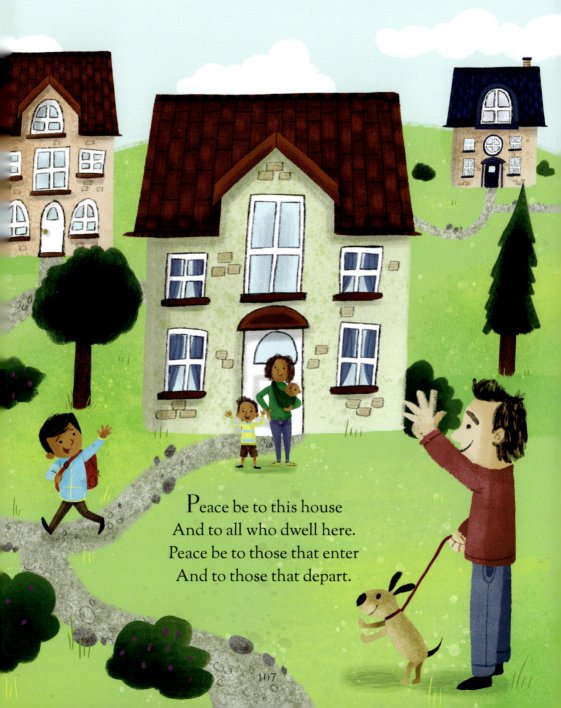

Peace be to this house
And to all who dwell here.
Peace be to those that enter
And to those that depart.

Grandma sits me on her knee,
Strokes my hair, and sings to me.

Grandpa jokes and plays baseball,
And picks me up when I fall.

At lunchtime, Grandpa likes to cook,
While Grandma sits and reads a book.
I love them, Lord, and pray that they
Will be there for me every day.

Dear God,
I kept a caterpillar in a jar
And it went into a little black cocoon.
I thought it was dead.
But, later, out of the cocoon
Came a beautiful butterfly.
Help me to remember
That people who die
Are a bit like my caterpillar.
In Your home in heaven,
They will be happy again,
Like beautiful butterflies.
Amen

Dear God,
If You are listening,
My granny died last night.
Mom says she's gone to heaven
And Dad said, "Yes, that's right."
So, God, if You should see her
In heaven up on high,
Tell her I shall miss her
And I'm sad to say goodbye.

Dear God,
Thank You for my family
and the things we do together.

Thank You for the meals we eat,
for the jokes we share,
for the bikes we ride,
and the place where we live.
Help us to remember
that we are part of Your family.

Look after my family
when we have to be apart.
Thank You for the thoughts we share,
the phone calls we make,
the memories we keep,
the prayers we pray.
Help us to remember
that You are with us all.
Amen

Help Me to Be Good

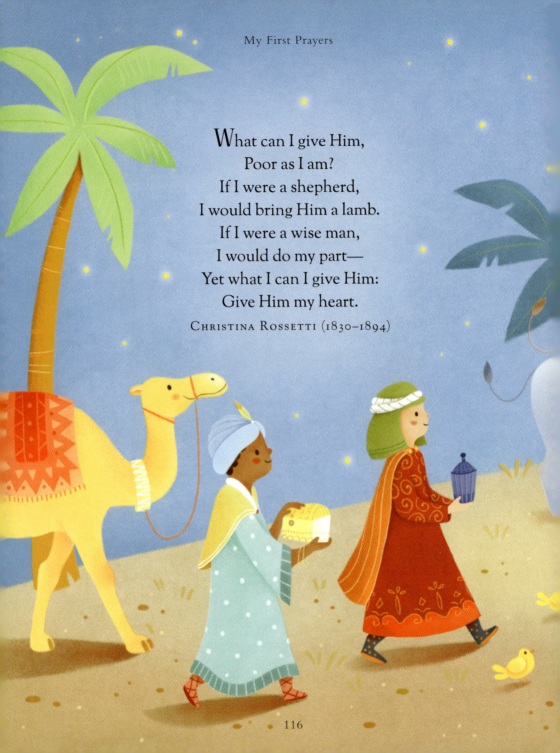

What can I give Him,
Poor as I am?
If I were a shepherd,
I would bring Him a lamb.
If I were a wise man,
I would do my part—
Yet what I can I give Him:
Give Him my heart.

Christina Rossetti (1830–1894)

Guide us, teach us, and strengthen us,
O Lord, we beseech Thee,
Until we become such as Thou would'st have us be:
Pure, gentle, truthful, high-minded,
Courteous, generous, able, dutiful, and useful;
For Thy honor and glory.

CHARLES KINGSLEY (1819–1875)

Lord, teach me all that I should know;
In grace and wisdom I may grow;
The more I learn to do Thy will,
The better may I love Thee still.

ISAAC WATTS (1674–1748)

Day by day, dear Lord, of Thee
Three things I pray:
To see Thee more clearly,
To love Thee more dearly,
To follow Thee more nearly,
Day by day.

St. Richard of Chichester (1197–1253)

O God, make us children of quietness and heirs of peace.
Amen

<small>St. Clement (First century)</small>

Last night, when I went to sleep,
I prayed that You would help me keep
A promise that I made to Mom
Not to be so quarrelsome.

I've really tried so hard today
To keep the promise, come what may,
And, Jesus, You will never guess
I think I've managed, more or less!

Dear God,
I think I'll help more
And give my mom some pleasure.
I'll tidy up my bedroom
And be her "little treasure."

Do other children help much?
Please tell me if they do,
And I'll make a special effort
For Mom and Dad and You.

Dear God,
I'm going to really try
To be good as good all day
And nice to all my special friends
When I go out to play.
If they say nasty things to me,
I mustn't do the same.
I don't want Mom to tell me off,
Or worse—give me the blame!
But, God, it isn't easy
To be as nice as pie,
So I know that You will help me
To really, really try!

Jesus, may I walk Your way
(point to feet)

in all I do
(hold out hands)

and all I say.
(touch finger to lips)
Amen

126

This is me
Looking up at You.
Help me
Always be
Close to You.

Help me to notice
when people need a hand.
Help me to see when they are sad
and need a friend.

Keep me from being
too busy to see
when someone needs a little help
from someone like me.

Sometimes, I'm good,
but I can be bad.
Sometimes, I'm happy;
sometimes, I'm sad.

I can be helpful,
I can be mean.
Sometimes, I'm somewhere
in between.
Help me to do what I know I should do.
Help me to choose to be good like You.

Dear God,
Help me to be good
when I have to share my toys.
Help me to be good
when I'm making too much noise.
Help me to be good
and eat up all my greens.
Help me to be good
when I'm tempted to be mean.
Help me to be good
each and every day.
Help me to be good
in every single way.
Amen

Make me pure, Lord: thou art holy;
Make me meek, Lord: thou wert lowly.

Gerard Manley Hopkins (1844–1889)

It's a Special Day

Our Father in heaven,
Hallowed be Your name.
Your kingdom come,
Your will be done,
On Earth as it is in heaven.
Give us today our daily bread,
And forgive us our sins,
As we forgive those who sin against us.
And lead us away from temptation
And deliver us from evil,
For Yours is the kingdom,
And the power, and the glory,
Forever and ever.
Amen

Christ be with me and within me;
Christ behind me;
Christ to win me;
Christ to comfort and restore me;
Christ beneath me;
Christ above me;
Christ in quiet and in danger;
Christ in hearts of all that love me;
Christ in mouth of friend and stranger.

ST. PATRICK (389–461)

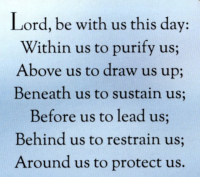

Lord, be with us this day:
Within us to purify us;
Above us to draw us up;
Beneath us to sustain us;
Before us to lead us;
Behind us to restrain us;
Around us to protect us.

St. Patrick (389–461)

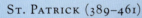

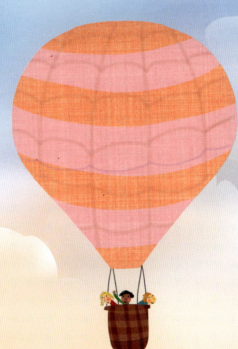

God be in my head,
And in my understanding;
God be in my eyes,
And in my looking;
God be in my mouth,
And in my speaking;
God be in my heart,
And in my thinking;
God be at my end,
And at my departing.

The Sarum Primer

Let the words of my mouth,
and the meditation of my heart,
be acceptable in Thy sight, O Lord,
my strength, and my redeemer.

PSALM 19

Can I see another's woe,
And not be in sorrow, too?
Can I see another's grief,
And not seek for kind relief?

WILLIAM BLAKE (1757–1827)

Let us with a gladsome mind
Praise the Lord for He is kind;
For His mercies shall endure,
Ever faithful, ever sure.

John Milton (1608–1674)

Dear God,
This is Monday.
Help me to start a good week.
Amen

Dear God,
It's Tuesday.
It's still early in the week.
Be with me as I try to make it a good one.
Amen

Dear God,
Wednesday already!
Midway through the week.
Please bless all those I meet today.
Amen

Dear God,
Thank You for Thursday.
I've made a good start.
Please help me with the rest of the week.
Amen

Dear God,
It's Friday.
Nearly the weekend!
Time to look back on my week.
Thank You for being with me.
Amen

Dear God,
It's Saturday—yippeee!
So much to do; so little time.
Please bless all of my friends today.
Amen

Dear God,
It's Sunday, Your day.
Happy day. Holy day.
Thank You for the week just gone.
Please help me to enjoy next week with You.
Amen

Sunday should be a fun day,
not a glum day.
Sunday should be a rest day,
not a work day.

When God finished making the world,
He had a rest, put up His feet,
And said, "That's good!"
Dear God, thank You for this Sunday.
Help us to rest and play,
To celebrate and say, "That's good!"

Today is a day to remember—
I finally pulled out my loose tooth!
I feel more grown up already.
Thank You, God, for special days to remember.
Amen

Here is the church,
(link hands)
Here is the steeple,
(put index fingers together)
Look inside,
(keeping your hands linked,
turn them upside down)
Here are the people!
(wiggle your fingers)

The things, good Lord, that we pray for,
give us grace to work for;
through Jesus Christ our Lord.

SIR THOMAS MORE (1478–1535)

These candles on my cake,
I blow them out,
A wish I make.
To this wish,
I add a prayer:
Please, God, be with me
Everywhere.

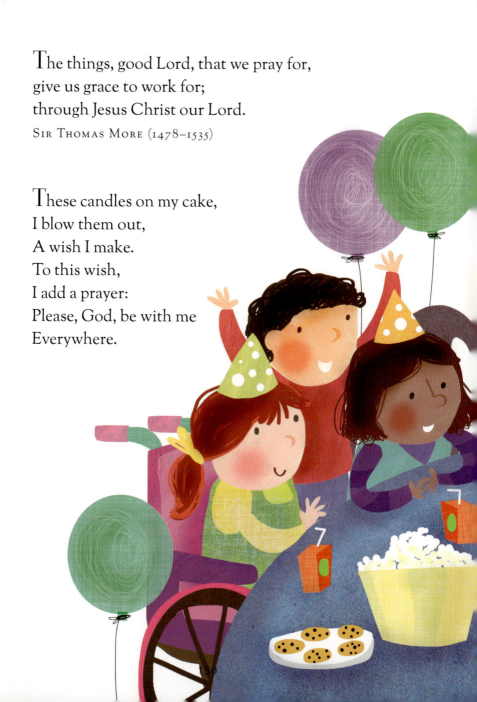

Dear Jesus,
Everyone thought you were dead.
They took you down from the cross, with tears in their eyes,
and buried you in a cave with a big stone outside.
Then they went home—the saddest people on Earth.

Later, they went back
to take flowers, but they got such a shock.
The stone was rolled away, the cave was empty,
and you were walking in the garden.
Then, they were the happiest people on Earth.
No wonder we are happy at Easter.
We know that you're alive
and always will be.

Happy birthday, Jesus!
Thank you for sharing your special day with us.
The Wise Men brought you gifts,
so we give presents.
Your family was happy,
and we have parties and food.
Thank you for giving us Christmas.
Happy birthday, Jesus!

We've been packing our stuff;
we've been counting the days;
we've been saying goodbye
in a whole lot of ways.
It's a very special day—we're moving!

Please travel with us
as we leave our old home.
Please help us to know
that we're never alone.

Now I'm Going to Sleep

Now the daylight goes away,
Savior, listen while I pray.
Asking Thee to watch and keep,
And to send me quiet sleep.

Jesus, Savior, wash away
All that has been wrong today:
Help me every day to be
Good and gentle, more like Thee.

REV. WILLIAM HENRY HAVERGAL (1793–1870)

160

When in the night I sleepless lie,
My soul with heavenly thoughts supply;
Let no ill dreams disturb my rest,
No powers of darkness me molest.

Praise God, from whom all blessings flow;
Praise Him all creatures here below,
Praise Him above, ye heavenly host;
Praise Father, Son and Holy Ghost.

BISHOP THOMAS KEN (1637–1711)

Matthew, Mark, Luke, and John,
Bless the bed that I lie on.
Four corners to my bed,
Four angels round my head,
One to watch and one to pray,
And two to bear my soul away.

God bless this house from roof to floor,
The twelve apostles guard the door;
Four angels to my bed;
Gabriel stands at the head,
John and Peter at the feet,
All to watch me while I sleep.

Hush! my dear, lie still and slumber,
Holy angels guard thy bed!
Heavenly blessings without number,
Gently falling on thy head.

Sleep, my babe; thy food and raiment,
House and home, thy friends provide;
All without thy care or payment,
All thy wants are well supplied.

How much better thou'rt attended
Than the Son of God could be,
When from heaven He descended
And became a child like thee!

Soft and easy is thy cradle:
Coarse and hard thy Savior lay:
When His birthplace was a stable,
And His softest bed was hay.

Isaac Watts (1674–1748)

Ah, dearest Jesus, holy child,
Make thee a bed, soft, undefiled
Within my heart, that it may be
A quiet chamber kept for thee.

MARTIN LUTHER (1483–1546)

I see the Moon,
And the Moon sees me;
God bless the Moon,
And God bless me.

Gentle Jesus, hear me,
Will you please be near me?
I don't want to be alone,
Feeling sad all on my own.
Tomorrow will be different
At the start of a new day,
But until the morning comes,
Stay close to me, I pray.

Dear God,
I'm staying over with my friend tonight,
We'll have a terrific time and not fight.
We'll eat too much; we'll laugh with glee.
So, when You come to look for me,
I won't be in my bed;
I'll be with my friend instead.

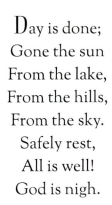

Day is done;
Gone the sun
From the lake,
From the hills,
From the sky.
Safely rest,
All is well!
God is nigh.

Sleep, my child, and peace attend thee,
All through the night;
Guardian angels God will send thee,
All through the night;

Soft the drowsy hours are creeping,
Hill and vale in slumber sleeping,
I, my loving vigil keeping,
All through the night.

TRADITIONAL WELSH PRAYER

Watch, O Lord,
with those who wake,
or watch or weep tonight,
and give your angels charge
over those who sleep.
Tend your sick ones,
O Lord Jesus Christ;
rest your weary ones;
bless your dying ones;
soothe your suffering ones;
pity your afflicted ones;
shield your joyous ones;
and all for your love's sake.

St. Augustine of Hippo (354–430)

Lord, keep us safe this night,
Secure from all our fears;
May angels guard us while we sleep,
Till morning light appears.

JOHN LELAND (1754–1841)

Now I lay me down to sleep,
I pray Thee, Lord, Thy child to keep:
Thy love guard me through the night
And wake me with the morning light.

Jesus, please be near me as I lie in bed tonight:
There's a dark place in the corner, and it's giving me a fright!
Mom says it's just a shadow, and shadows are thin air,
But I can see it grinning, and it's sitting in my chair!
Please shine your light, dear Jesus, so that I can see
The shadow's really nothing now you are close to me.

When I put my hands together,
When I say a prayer,
When I stop and say Your name,
You are there.

When I'm frightened of the dark,
When I've had a scare,
When I think I'm all alone,
You are there.

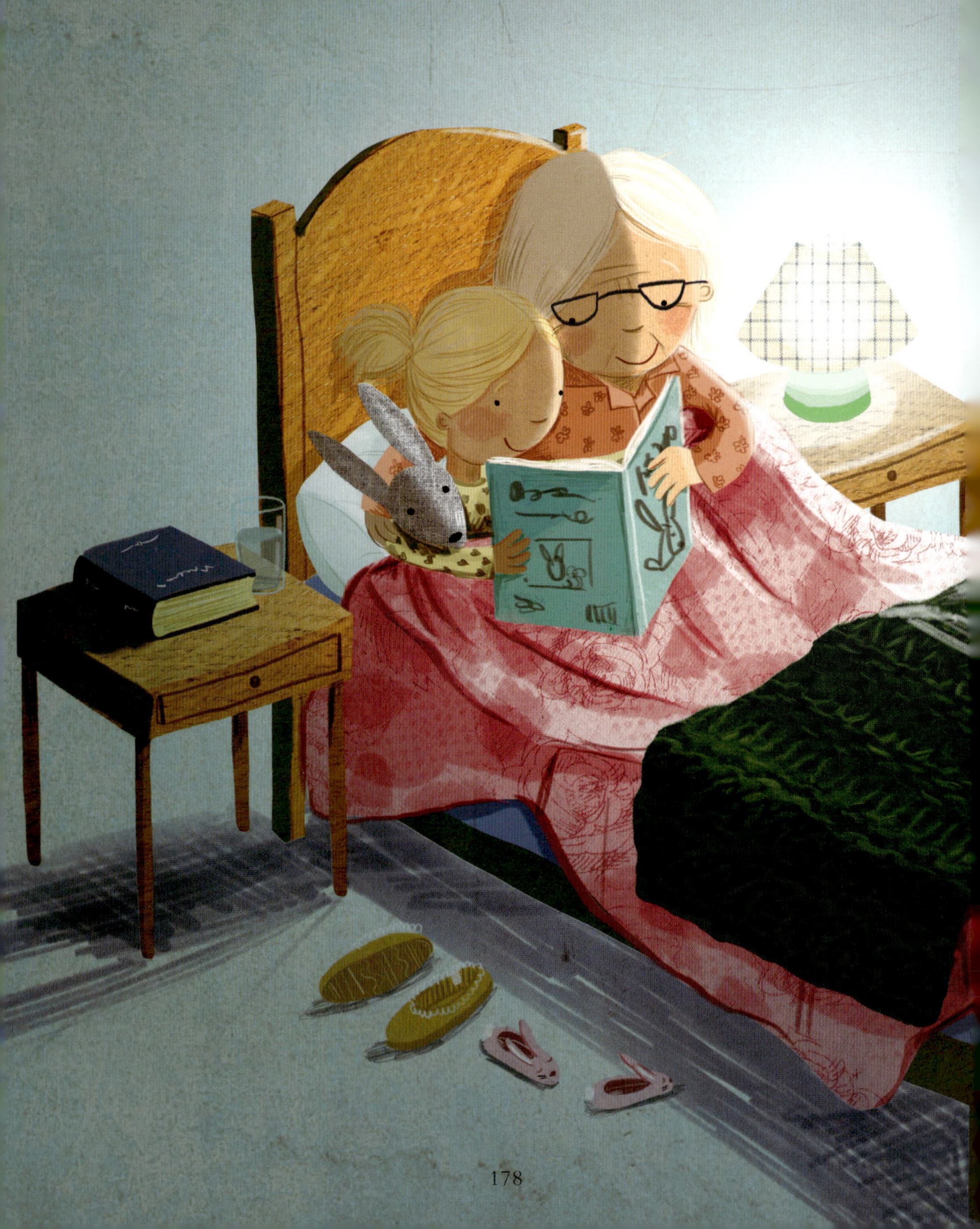

I'm sleeping at my grandma's,
And I miss my mom and dad.
But Grandma cooked my favorite meal,
And now I'm not so sad!

I like to sleep at Grandma's;
She says it makes her glad.
Please, God, bless my grandma,
And bless my mom and dad.

It's time to sleep.
I've brushed my teeth
and read my book,
I've put my robe
on the hook,
and—

I just can't sleep.
The bed's too hot,
the light's too bright,
there's far too many
sounds tonight,
but—

I still can't sleep.
I've shut my eyes,
I've said a prayer,
"God bless children
everywhere,"
then—

Perhaps I'll sleep.
I think I might.
I think I'll—yawn—
turn out the light.
Good night.
Zzzzz...

Good night! Good night!
Far flies the light;
But still God's love
Shall flame above,
Making all bright.
Good night! Good night!

VICTOR HUGO (1802–1885)

The Moon shines bright,
The stars give light
Before the break of day;
God bless you all
Both great and small
And send a joyful day.

Index of Prayers